NOT ME!

by

Bil Keane

FAWCETT GOLD MEDAL • NEW YORK

NOT ME!

© 1976 The Register & Tribune Syndicate, Inc.

© 1980 The Register & Tribune Syndicate, Inc.

Published by special arrangement with The Register & Tribune
Syndicate, Inc. by Fawcett Gold Medal Books, a unit of CBS
Publications, the Consumer Publishing Division of CBS Inc.

ISBN 0-449-14333-3

Printed in the United States of America

First Fawcett Gold Medal printing: April 1980

10 9 8 7 6 5 4

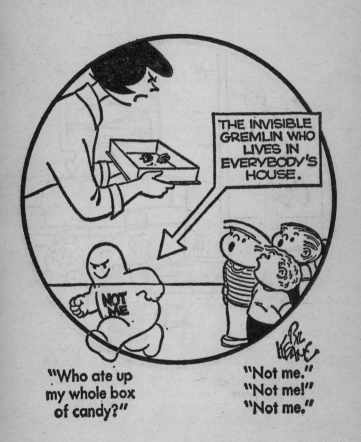

"Okay, who
did it?"

"Not me."
"Not me."

"Who dirtied this
clean towel?"

"Not me."
"Not me."

"Daddy! Remember when you said you'd help
us build a snowman next time
it snowed? . . ."

"Buildin' this snowman won't take long, Daddy, 'cause you have plenty of help!"

"Wow! Do you know how to build a whole
snowman without readin' any
'structions, Daddy?"

"No, Daddy! Let's make him a NON-SMOKER so he'll last longer!"

"Now, can we make him a snow LADY so he won't be lonely?"

"He can't hear us any more Jeffy. He's dead."

"Who tracked in
all this mud?"

"Not me!"
"Not me!"

"I can't go over to Jimmy's house 'cause I
can't find his sidewalk."

"Billy got a Valentine! Billy got a Valentine!"

"We wanna have a snowball fight, Daddy.
Will you make 'em for us?"

"When you write fast your words get mumbly."

"Mommy, your eyes are bigger than my stomach."

"I put in some of my bubble bath to make everything smell nice."

"Daddy's mowing the snow!"

"That's very good, Grandma, but you forgot
to color the duck's beak."

"I'm glad Mommy doesn't have whiskers. If she did we'd NEVER get breakfast."

"Daddy does that 'Fe, Fi, Fo, Fum' part better."

"Don't use that wash cloth, Mommy. That's
the one the sitter used last night to wipe
up after Barfy."

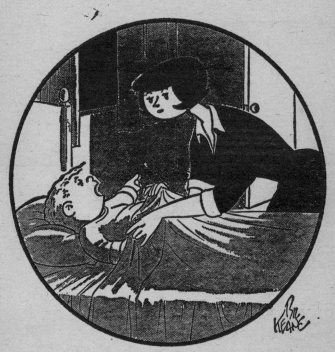

• "You and Daddy aren't goin' out, are you?"

"Guess what my favorite color is. I'll give you a hint — it's red."

"Mommy, have you retired from having babies?"

"Billy says he doesn't hafta go to church tomorrow 'cause he's listening to 'Dial-A-Prayer' on the phone."

"You're not s'posed to eat anything near Daddy while he's on his diet!"

"Zip up your jacket, Billy—— you've had a cold.
And, here —— use this tissue."

"I marked my lunch for school, Mommy."

"G'night, Joey, g'night, Charlie, g'night, Mir-
anda, g'night, Jaws, g'night, Freddy,
g'night. . . ."

"I'm not even using a flashbulb this time!"

"Daddy said he bought us a new pet, but it's nothin' but a plain ol' ROCK!"

"But what's it s'posed to DO? It just SITS there!"

"I like our pet rabbit better than our pet rock."

"They're callin' it 'Pete the Rock'! I wanted it to be a GIRL!"

"It's MY turn to sleep with Pete the Rock!"

"I brought in a few friends for our pet rock
to play with."

"How'd the doorknob get so sticky?"

"That's funny — it always spells okay for Mommy."

"How did you know what my name was when I was borned?"

"No, she's not busy, Grandma."

"Mommy'll find it. She's a better looker than Daddy."

"Who's been writing
on the car?"

"Not me."
"Not me!"

"Mommy, is this a 'P' or a 'Q'?"

"Was the wheel to my fire engine in last week's trash?"

"Her real name is Thelma. 'Mommy' is just her nickname."

"Grandma doesn't just have ROUND
crackers. She has square ones and
triangle ones and . . ."

"Well, if I carry one of the packages, THEN
can you carry me?"

"But Daddy's boss is just comin' over to see
HIM! Why does EVERYBODY have to
get cleaned up?"

"He's here, Mommy! Shall I let him in or are
you still cleanin' up?"

"We can't put your coat and hat in the closet
'cause that's where we shoved everything
before you came."

"Are you stayin' for dinner?"

"Why didn't your mommy come with you?"

"I wanted to show you my room but Mommy said 'DON'T YOU DARE!'"

"I like the way they put each thing in its own little yard."

"Mrs. Tippit must be a good mommy 'cause she smiles a lot."

"Can we go down the cookie aisle first?"

"Daddy, am I talkin' in your sleep?"

"If we ask you something will you say 'yes'?"

"How come we hardly ever get to eat in the dining room?"

"Well, what did you learn in school today?"
"Never put marshmallows in back pockets."

"Want me to read you awake?"

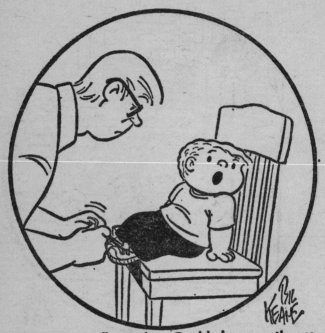

"Mommy, will you show Daddy how we tie my laces in a double knot?"

"Mommy! Jeffy used up the whole roll again!"

"The doorbell stopped ringing, Mommy. Do I
still have to answer it for you?"

"If a lady calls you 'bout somethin,' Mommy, I
didn't mean it!"

"I'll hold the umbrella if you'll walk bent over
for a while."

"They make it that way so you can't slam it."

"Who's been jumping
in this hedge?"

"Not me."
"Not me."

"I think we're in trouble — Mommy's mouth is getting mad."

"Where's my baseball mitt? I just saw a robin!"

"Mommy! The soup's tryin' to get out!"

"I'll wash, you dry."

"Shh! If you scare them they'll go back under-
ground."

"But, Mommy! How you s'posed to stop a sneeze?"

"Red means stop, and green means go, and yellow means hurry up."

"I owe you a kiss! The bus is coming!"

"Because I'm not READY to go home, that's why!"

"Who left my racket
out in the rain?"

"Not me."
"Not me!"

"Mommy, can I get one of those hats with the shelf in front?"

"Don't let Barfy out! He'll get blamed for upsetting everybody's trash cans!"

"You can't read this, PJ! It's an ADULT book — it has WORDS in it."

"Mommy, the toast is ready for scraping."

"He has his own camper."

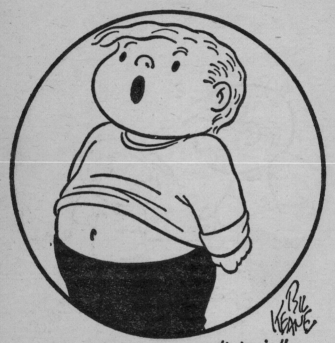

"Mommy, my tummy won't stay in."

"I could have caught it, but I didn't want to."

"I'll go wake Daddy up, okay?"

"Look, Mommy — North Knee Island and
South Knee Island."

"That's a bruise, not a bad spot."

"I'm SUPPOSED to take it when I jump it."

"Peter Piper picked a peck of pickled peppers,
a peck of pickled peppers Peter Piper
picked . . ."

"Psst, fly! This way out!"

"Know what I like about clouds? You can draw them any shape you want."

"Wanna help me set the lawn for croquet?"

"Know what? The man next door is paintin' his garage."

"Do you have to bleed for it to be a real cut finger?"

" 'Alleluia' is the old-fashioned way of saying 'Hooray.' "

"WOW! A RABBIT, and it's LIVE! No batter-
ies, no wind-up or anything! Can we keep it?"

"Gee, Daddy. I wish you'd have gotten a
bunny rabbit for EACH of us!"

"But, how can we name it if we don't know
whether it's a boy or a girl?"

"No Barfy! No! It's okay — Snowball is one of the family!"

"Put him down, Jeffy!
It's not good for
rabbits to be
handled!"

"I'm hungry, Mommy — could I have a piece of lettuce?"

"He LIKES me! He's wagging his nose!"

"We hope you remembered to buy carrots!"

"Wanna hold him, Grandma? Don't worry —
he won't bite."

"I heard him thumping for me to come down
and give him a hug."

"Speak! Come on, Snowball, speak!"

"Aren't you real glad you bought us a bunny
rabbit, Daddy?"

"I'll take Snowball in to watch TV while you clean out his cage, Mommy."

"Who had my pinking shears?"
"Ida Know."

"Who's responsible for the lumps of jelly mixed
in with the peanut butter?"
"Ida Know."

"Who crossed out 'broccoli' on my grocery list?"

"Ida know." "Ida know." "Ida know."

"The hinges on my roll broke."

"Grandma, will YOU read me a story?"

"It means we have to take a long cut."

"We won't have any dessert 'cause we always
stop for ice cream cones on the way home."

"Ow! Ouch! Don't put me down! The sand's HOT!"

"It's not heated!"

"Boy! The TV programs on vacation aren't as
good as the ones we watch at home."

"Okay, who threw the frisbee?"
"Ida Know."
"Not me."

"Is it okay to play in the suds?"

"You don't have to show me how to do it — I already know how they work."

"Who brought all this sand up from the
beach?"

"Ida Know."

"Not me."

Have Fun with the Family Circus

☐	ANY CHILDREN?	14116	$1.50
☐	DADDY'S LITTLE HELPERS	14384	$1.50
☐	DOLLY HIT ME BACK!	14273	$1.50
☐	GOOD MORNING SUNSHINE!	14356	$1.50
☐	FOR THIS I WENT TO COLLEGE?	14069	$1.50
☐	NOT ME!	14333	$1.50
☐	I'M TAKING A NAP	14144	$1.50
☐	LOOK WHO'S HERE	14207	$1.50
☐	PEACE, MOMMY, PEACE	14145	$1.50
☐	PEEKABOO! I LOVE YOU!	14174	$1.50
☐	WANNA BE SMILED AT?	14118	$1.50
☐	WHEN'S LATER, DADDY?	14124	$1.50
☐	MINE	14056	$1.50
☐	SMILE!	14172	$1.50
☐	JEFFY'S LOOKIN' AT ME!	14096	$1.50
☐	CAN I HAVE A COOKIE?	14155	$1.50
☐	THE FAMILY CIRCUS	14068	$1.50
☐	HELLO, GRANDMA?	14169	$1.50
☐	I NEED A HUG	14147	$1.50
☐	QUIET! MOMMY'S ASLEEP!	13030	$1.50

Buy them at your local bookstore or use this handy coupon for ordering.

COLUMBIA BOOK SERVICE, CBS Publications
32275 Mally Road, P.O. Box FB, Madison Heights, MI 48071

Please send me the books I have checked above. Orders for less than 5 books must include 75¢ for the first book and 25¢ for each additional book to cover postage and handling. Orders for 5 books or more postage is FREE. Send check or money order only. Allow 3-4 weeks for delivery.

Cost $_____   Name _____

Sales tax*_____   Address _____

Postage_____   City _____

Total $_____   State _____ Zip _____

* The government requires us to collect sales tax in all states except AK, DE, MT, NH and OR.

Prices and availability subject to change without notice.